Table of Contents

ISBN: 978-1-7368260-0-3

KIDVE$TORS™

What is Real Estate?

Real estate is any immovable property such as land, homes, and buildings.

Check the box that is NOT Real estate

Question #1

A. **HOUSE**

B. **LAND**

C. **CAR**

D. **STORE**

Discussion

Why do you think investing in real estate is important?

Crossword Puzzle!

Complete the crossword puzzle by filling in the appropriate letters with the help of hints listed below

Across

3. Money leftover every month from rental property

5. The owner has to pay as long as they own the property

Down

1. A loan from a bank that is used to buy a house or building

2. Someone who determines what a house is worth

4. This is when you buy a house to only make repairs and sell for a high price

What is Property Value?

Property value is a number that determines what a piece of land or property is worth. An appraiser is someone who determines the value.

Question #1

Appraised Value

180,000.00

The house above is valued at $150,000.00.

Check the box with the correct option.

☐ **True**

☐ **False**

Question #2

Check the box with the correct option.

What is an Appraiser?

☐ **A.** Someone who Sells Houses

☐ **B.** Someone who repairs Houses

☐ **C.** Someone who determines what a house is worth

☐ **D.** Someone who buys Houses

What is Appreciation?

Appreciation is when real estate grows in value in a neighborhood over time. Appreciation is not guaranteed and is based off of the location and sales of other homes in the neighborhood.

Question #1

$180,000.00

$190,000.00

How much did the home appreciate
(Grow) in 2 years?

$ [   ]

Find all of the words that are written below.

```
P J T E R R I T O R Y
F O R E C L O S U R E
N D T L L K N K C T E
J L U M A B N N L K Q
W V K P H N K N O M U
N D P Z L B D S S D I
W T B D L E E I I M T
Z T N Y M S X B N G Y
L A V L U C H N G G L
L P Z O R W W W H Z S
Z V H N C Y X P R T M
```

Closing	Foreclosure	Landings
Duplex	Houses	Territory
Equity	Land	

Read the sentence and circle the correct answer.

Check the box with the correct option.

Appreciation Is Always Guaranteed.

☐ **True**

☐ **False**

Carrying costs are also called holding costs. Carrying (or holding) costs are costs that an owner has to pay as long as they own the property. Carrying costs can include: a mortgage, utilities, property taxes, and insurance. Owners who are landlords can pass along their carrying costs to their tenants. It's important for homeowners to remember carrying costs so that they can budget properly and make sure that they have enough money for all expenses.

Question #1

Which of the following are considered real estate carrying costs?

Property Taxes

Insurance

Groceries

Car Note

Gas

Mortgage

Help DJ Find the treasure!

Question #2

Discussion

Why is it important to know your carrying costs?

What is Mortgage, Interest, and a Down Payment?

A mortgage is a loan from a bank that is used to buy a house or building. The loan is paid back monthly over time with an additional fee called interest. A down payment is a lump sum of money that is paid first and subtracted from the loan. What is leftover is the mortgage.

Question #1

DJ & Averie's parents borrowed **$150,000.00** to buy a home and will pay an additional **$20,000.00** in interest. How much will their total mortgage be?

$ [   ]

Solve the word problem. For the first blank, write your answer from Question 1 in Lesson 5.

A. DJ and Averie's parents' mortgage was?

= [   ]

B. They paid $30,000 as a down payment. How much of the mortgage do they have left to pay?

= [   ]

Crossword Puzzle!

Complete the crossword puzzle by filling in the appropriate letters with the help of hints listed below

Across

2. A legal document proving ownership of real estate
5. A service such as light, power, or water
6. Someone who sells houses

Down

1. The amount of money left over after expenses
3. A person who pays monthly to live in a property
4. A number that determines what a piece of real estate is worth

What are Utilities, Property taxes, and Insurance?

Utilities are recurring costs that homeowners have to pay monthly such as electricity, gas, water, sewage, and garbage disposal.

Property tax is a type of tax (or fee) charged by your state and county for owning a property. Property taxes must be paid in full by the end of every year.

Homeowner's insurance is a monthly cost paid by a homeowner to cover the cost for major damages or repairs that may be needed for the property.

Read the statement and check the correct option.

Question #1

Check the box with the correct option. ✔

☐ **True**

☐ **False**

Property taxes are monthly costs paid by a homeowner to cover the cost of major damages.

List four different types of utilities:

#1 _____

#2 _____

#3 _____

#4 _____

Multiple choice. Check all of the correct answers.

Check the box with the correct option.

DJ and Averie's parents had a leak in their kitchen then discovered that their roof needed to be repaired. Which option can they use to cover the cost?

A. Property Taxes

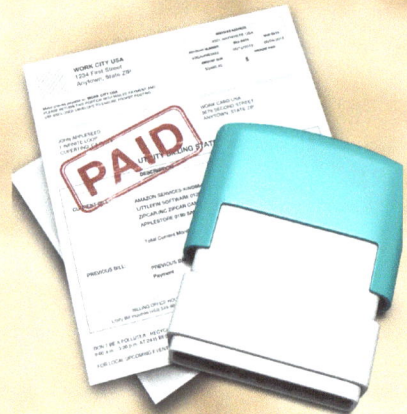

B. Utilities

C. Commissions

D. Insurance

KIDVE$TORS™

What is Equity?

Equity is the difference between a property's value and the mortgage left on the property.

Solve the word problem.
For the first blank, write your answer from Lesson 5, 2B

Question #1

DJ and Averie's parents owe [blank] on the mortgage after they paid their down payment. The home's value is worth **$180,000.00**.

How much equity does DJ and Averie's home have?

Property Value = 180,000.00

Mortgage $ [blank]

Equity $ [blank]

Maze

Help Averie find her bag of Gold!

What is the best way to buy a home with equity?

What is a Rental Property?

A rental property is a property where the owner collects money every month from tenants. Owners who have tenants are called Landlords. Tenants are people who pay rent (a monthly fee) to live in the property.

Question #1

Solve the word problem.

DJ and Averie's family owns Rental Property #1 with 2 tenants.

Each tenant pays **$800.00** per month.

How much in rent do DJ & Averie's family collect every month?

$800.00 + $800.00

$ [   ]

Solve the word problem. For the first blank, write your answer from Question 1, Lesson 8.

DJ and Averie's parents own two rental properties.

Property #1 collects _____ per month.

Property #2 collects **$2,000.00** per month. How much total rental income do they collect every month?

Draw a line to match the words with the correct statement.

Landlord

A person who pays rent monthly to live in a property.

Tenant

A person who owns A property and collects rent.

What is Profit and Cash flow?

Profit is the amount of money left over after expenses. Cash flow is the money left over every month from a rental property. An investor should only buy a rental property that cash flows.

Question #1

Solve the word Problem

DJ and Averie's rental property costs and expenses for Property #1 is **$1,000.00** every month. Based on the rent collected, what is the amount of profit they have left over every month? In the first blank insert your answer from Question #1 in Lesson 8.

Rent Collected

Expenses

Monthly cash flow

DJ and Averie's parents are looking to buy another rental property. The rent collected every month will be **$800.00**, but the expenses every month will be **$1,000.00**. Should DJ and Averie's parents buy this rental property?

Why or Why not?

Activity

Word Search

Find all of the words that are written below.

```
L D G R R R V W F Y L H L
P R O P E R T Y V A L U E
A P P R E C I A T I O N E
F Q I R D N R P M X L G M
G T K N M L W M M F A Y I
R R L D S F M E N G D B N
Q E N M J U C R T L T K V
X N A G W N R R G C L L E
N N D L A T O A H L H M S
Z T H N T M V J N Y K T T
Y H I K K O X W K C B K O
Q F H K V Q R C P R E C R
L C O N T R A C T O R L C
```

Finance	Property Value	Appreciation
Contractor	Mortgage	Insurance
Realtor		Investor

What is Flipping?

Flipping is when you buy a house at a low price, make repairs and improvements, then sell for a higher price.

Question #1

When you buy a house to flip, should you buy at a high price or low price?

☐ **High Price**

☐ **Low Price**

Solve The Word Problem.

DJ and Averie's parents bought a house for **$100,000.00.** They spent $30,000.00 on repairs. After the repairs were completed, they sold the house for **$200,000.00.** What was their profit?

Crossword Puzzle!

Down

I. When real estate grows in value over time
2. This is the final step for ownership of the property transferred to the buyer

Across

3. A scheduled time for a viewing by potential buyers
4 This person takes care of selling the property
5. Someone who is licensed to renovate or build houses

What is a Title and Deed?

A title is a legal document proving ownership of real estate. A deed is a legal document showing the transfer of title from the previous owner to a new owner.

Check the box with the correct option.

Question #1

A title is a legal document showing the transfer of ownership from the previous owner to a new owner.

☐ **True**

☐ **False**

Question #2

Discussion

Why is it important to have the title and deed when you buy a home?

Find all of the words that are written below.

```
K V C R N R N T L Y G N
H I N V E S T M E N T E
I N S P E C T I O N T I
K S K L N Q E N G D Q G
F N E M M T G D E F Y H
H D H L A Y M E T M V B
T T E T L J D N N R L O
D G S P B E L N V K V R
B E B R O G R D P T R H
R P G F R S M Z T R K O
W R C K R L I R Y M B O
R R E N T A L T D K G D
```

Deed   Inspection   Rental

Deposit   Investment   Seller

Estate   Neighborhood

What is a Realtor?

A Realtor is a man or woman who is licensed to buy and sell real estate. A Realtor earns their living by taking a commission on the sale of each home. A Realtor can help an investor buy or sell property, but it is not a requirement.

Question #1

A Realtor has a license to repair and renovate homes. True or False?

Check the box with the correct option.

☐ **True**

☐ **False**

Check the box with the correct option.

Investors have to use a Realtor to buy and sell property.

☐ True

☐ False

35

Lesson 13

What is a General Contractor?

A General Contractor is a man or woman who is licensed to renovate or build houses.

Question #1

A General Contractor is licensed to sell homes. True or False?

Check the box with the correct option.

☑

☐ **True**

☐ **False**

X Marks the spot! Can you help DJ find the right path!

A General Contractor asked DJ and Averie's parents to renovate one of their rental properties, but he was not licensed. Should they use this General Contractor? Why or why not?

Activity

Matching

Draw a line to match the words with the correct statements.

Realtor

The amount of money left over after expenses.

General Contractor

A legal document showing the transfer of title from the previous owner to the new owner.

Title

A man or woman who is licensed to repair or renovate houses.

Deed

A legal document showing ownership of real estate.

Profit

A man or woman who is licensed to sell real estate.

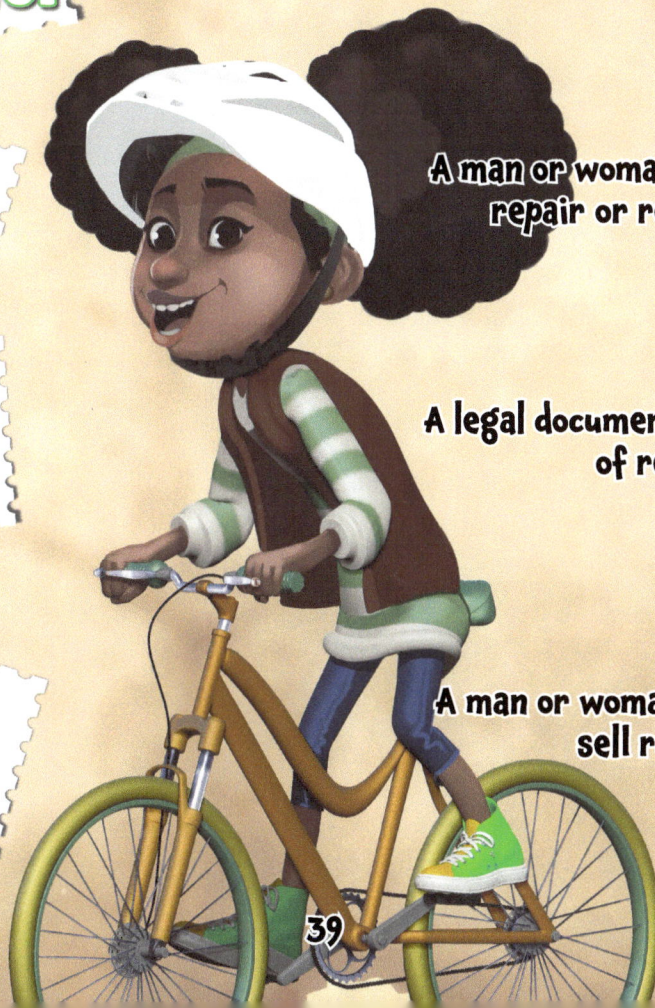

39

What is Financial Freedom?

Financial freedom is when you and your family have created enough wealth to control your time.

Question #1

How does investing in real estate help you achieve financial freedom?

Find all of the words that are written below.

```
T N T H L Y M F K N Z H
P I M T W X B K R G W O
K L T U Z V L E N H S M
R P L L T P S I C E Y E
M N R W E I P R S L G O
J M T T A P L N W V M W
M P D R I W E I N M V N
H K P L J P L T T V K E
C P F T X K C T K I R R
A D L E T L K P J D E S
F J G C A S H F L O W S
Y G K T A X E S K R K B
```

Appraiser

Cash flow

Expenses

Flipping

Home Owners

Taxes

Title

Utilities

Do you believe that you can achieve financial freedom?
If so, please tell us Why?

Sit down with your parents and begin making a plan on how to achieve financial freedom for your family.

Glossary

Appreciation

When real estate grows in value over time.

Carrying Costs

Carrying costs are also called holding costs. Carrying (or holding) costs are costs that an owner has to pay as long as they own the property.

Cash flow

Is the money left over every month from a rental property.

Deed

A legal document showing the transfer of title from the previous owner to the new owner.

Equity

The difference between a property's value and the amount of the mortgage or what you owe on the property.

Flipping

Buying a house at a low price, making repairs and improvement, then selling for a higher price.

General Contractor

A man or woman who is licensed to repair or renovate houses.

Insurance

Is a monthly cost paid by a homeowner to cover the cost for a major damages or repairs that may be needed for the property.

Interest

A loan paid back monthly over time with an additional fee

Mortgage

A loan from a bank used to buy a house or building. The loan is paid back over time with interest.

Profit

The amount of money left over after expenses.

Property Taxes

Is a type of tax (or fee) charged by your state and county for owning a property. Property taxes must be paid in full by the end of the year.

Glossary

Real Estate

Real estate is any immovable property such as land, homes, and buildings.

Realtor

A man or woman who is licensed to sell real estate. A Realtor earns their living by taking a commission on the sale of each home.

Rental Property

A property where the owner collects money every month from tenants. Tenants are people who pay rent (a monthly fee) to live in the property.

Title

A legal document showing ownership of real estate.

Utilities

Are recurring costs that homeowners have to pay monthly such as electricity, gas, water, sewage, and garbage disposal.

Value

A number that determines what a piece of real estate is worth.

A Quest for Hidden Treasures in REAL ESTATE

Enroll your student in the Kidvestors Real Estate Investing course!
www.kidvestorsacademy.com

Join their online community by following them on social media:

Instagram: thekidvestors
Facebook: Facebook.com/kidvestors
Twitter: Twitter.com/kidvestors

KIDVE$TORS™

Tgosketch Illustration
www.tgosketch.com

To purchase the book, visit us online at
www.TheKidvestors.com